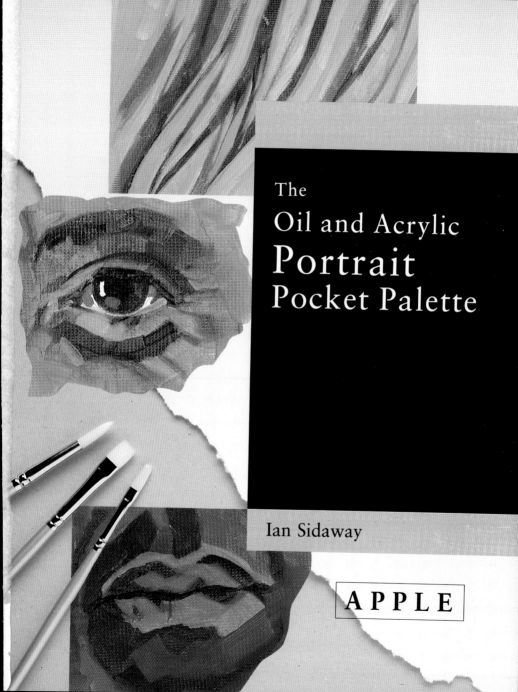

The

Oil and Acrylic
Portrait
Pocket Palette

Ian Sidaway

APPLE

A QUARTO BOOK

Published by The Apple Press
6 Blundell Street
London N7 9BH

ISBN 1-85076-722-X

This book was designed
and produced by
Quarto Publishing plc
6 Blundell Street
London N7 9BH

Art Director Moira Clinch
Senior Art Editor
Clare Baggaley
Designer Sallyann
Bradnam
Editorial Director
Mark Dartford
Senior Editor Sally
MacEachern
Editor Helen Douglas-
Cooper
Ilustrations Ian Siddaway
Picture Research
Giulia Hetherington

Typeset in Great Britain
by Genesis Typesetting
Manufactured by Bright
Arts
Pte Ltd, Singapore
Printed by Leefung-Asco
Printers, China

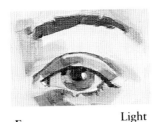

Eyes Light Medium

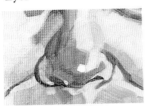

Noses Light Medium

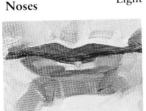

Mouths Light Medium

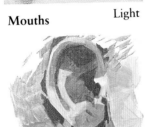

Ears Light Medium

Pulling it together Light Medium

CONTENTS

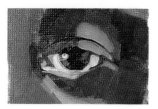

Dark

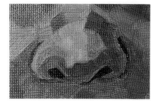

Dark

Dark

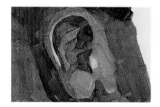

Dark

Dark

HOW TO USE THIS BOOK

THE AIM OF THIS BOOK is to provide the artist with an easy, at-a-glance guide to various colour and mixing combinations that between them cover a diverse range of skin colouring for different age groups. This book does not claim to cover all possibilities, but shows that even a limited range of colours can give a selection of possible mixes for light, medium and dark-skinned people. There is no correct way to paint flesh. Each artist finds his or her own approach, and you should always be prepared to experiment with different combinations of colours.

Structure

The book is divided into five sections. The first four focus on individual features – eyes, noses, mouths and ears. The final section shows you how to pull it all together as you paint the face and hair. Each section begins with a spread showing how light, angle and tone affect the way you see and paint features. This is followed by three spreads on painting light, medium and dark skins. The final section includes three extra spreads on painting hair.

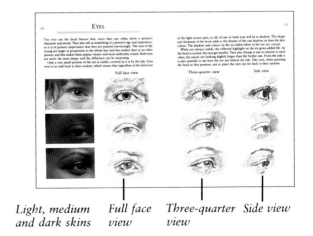

Light, medium and dark skins   *Full face view*   *Three-quarter view*   *Side view*

Light skin spread

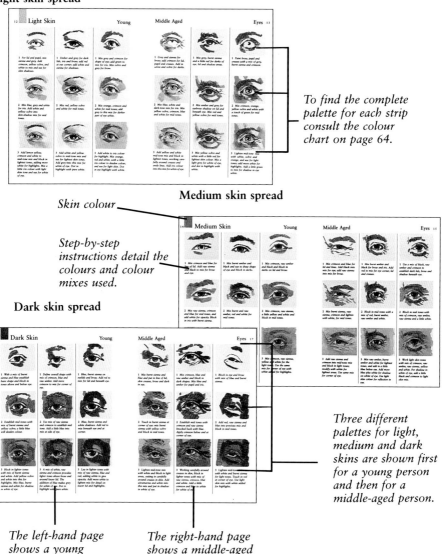

To *find* the complete palette for each strip consult the colour chart on page 64.

Skin colour

Medium skin spread

Step-by-step instructions detail the colours and colour mixes used.

Dark skin spread

Three different palettes for light, medium and dark skins are shown first for a young person and then for a middle-aged person.

The left-hand page shows a young person's features.

The right-hand page shows a middle-aged person's features.

SKIN COLOUR

Skin tones and colours can be mixed from many different tube colours. However, most professional artists tend to work with a palette of around ten or twelve colours and through experimentation they learn to mix all the colours they need. The ten colours below plus white make a good starter palette. Beneath are a few mixes using those basic colours.

Basic palette

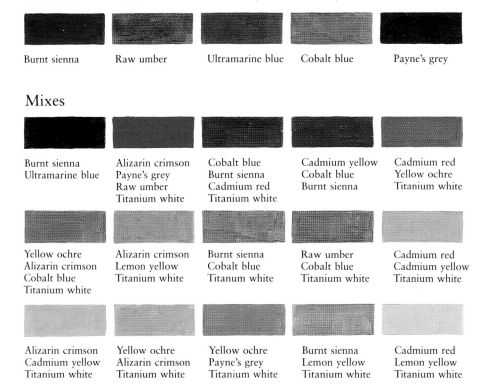

Cadmium red — Alizarin crimson — Cadmium yellow — Lemon yellow — Yellow ochre

Burnt sienna — Raw umber — Ultramarine blue — Cobalt blue — Payne's grey

Mixes

Burnt sienna
Ultramarine blue

Alizarin crimson
Payne's grey
Raw umber
Titanium white

Cobalt blue
Burnt sienna
Cadmium red
Titanium white

Cadmium yellow
Cobalt blue
Burnt sienna

Cadmium red
Yellow ochre
Titanium white

Yellow ochre
Alizarin crimson
Cobalt blue
Titanium white

Alizarin crimson
Lemon yellow
Titanium white

Burnt sienna
Cobalt blue
Titanum white

Raw umber
Cobalt blue
Titanium white

Cadmium red
Cadmium yellow
Titanium white

Alizarin crimson
Cadmium yellow
Titanium white

Yellow ochre
Alizarin crimson
Titanium white

Yellow ochre
Payne's grey
Titanium white

Burnt sienna
Lemon yellow
Titanium white

Cadmium red
Lemon yellow
Titanium white

The achromatic scale is a tonal scale that runs from black through grey to white in a series of slight, evenly graduated steps. All colours can be matched to a tonal value on this scale. Dark blue is close to black on the scale, as is dark red, but they are totally different colours. Look at a black and white photograph and you will see how colours assume a tonal value. An understanding of tonal value is central to good portrait painting if a correct degree of modelling is to be achieved. On an evenly lit face, the tonal values of colours are close together which will flatten it. If the face is lit from one side, that side will be light and the other side in shadow, resulting in a wide range of tonal values that makes the face more three-dimensional and gives a sense of drama. It is prudent to bear this in mind when posing your subject.

achromatic scale

skin tone

*Dramatic lighting makes
light skin look dark.*

*Reflected light makes dark
skin appear light in tone.*

TECHNIQUES

OIL PAINT IS the traditional portrait-painting medium. However, the same techniques that are used with oils can also be used with acrylic paint. The one unique characteristic of acrylic paint, its fast drying time, can easily be overcome by adding a retarder to the mix.

ALLA PRIMA

Working directly on to the support with little or no preliminary underdrawing and completing the painting in a single session is known as alla prima. The colours and tones are laid side by side, more or less as in the finished painting.

◄If the paint is mixed to a buttery consistency and applied wet into wet with quick clean strokes, an alla prima painting will have a lively surface texture showing the brushmarks left by the quick direct application of the paint.

GLAZING

Glazing consists of building up layers of transparent paint over an underpainting. Each layer of colour modifies and darkens the one beneath, giving colours a degree of luminosity and depth that is unobtainable by mixing colours on the palette.

*Glazing with oils is a slow process►
because each layer needs to dry
completely before the next is
applied. The process will be quicker
with acrylic as the paint dries fast.
Always use a glazing medium to
thin oil paint, not just turpentine.*

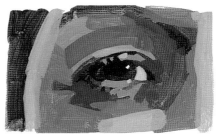

You can begin a portrait by making a tonal underpainting using just one colour; any neutral colour is suitable. Traditionally, terre verte was used, but raw sienna or Payne's grey are equally acceptable. Render the whole subject in light and dark tones, applying the paint thinly. When this layer is dry, rework the subject using the full palette of chosen colours. Quick-drying acrylic paint is ideal for the tonal underpainting.

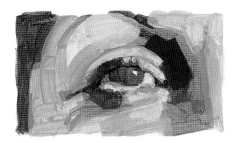

◄This process allows you to assess the image in two distinct phases: first as tone only, in order to check that you have got the balance of tones and degree of modelling that you want; then in terms of colour, the tonal values of which can be matched to the underpainting.

BLOCKING IN

Blocking in is a form of loose underpainting in which you treat the subject initially as a series of flat shapes, working across the whole painting in aproximately the right colours and tones using large brushes and thin paint. This allows you to assess and make changes to the composition and the basic drawing of the head before too much paint is applied. Continue the painting by building up form and colour, gradually reducing the size of the brushwork, and concentrating on the details last of all.

Acrylics are an ideal medium to use▶ for blocking in. You can make changes as you go and then complete the painting in either acrylics or oils. If you are using oils for blocking in, work with thinner paint and allow the paint to become thicker in the final working.

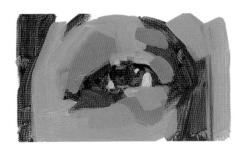

THE EYES ARE the facial feature that, more than any other, show a person's character and mood. They also tell us something of a person's age and experience, so it is of primary importance that they are painted convincingly. The eyes of the young are larger in proportion to the whole face and less sunken than in an older person, and this makes them appear clearer and more uniformly round. Both eyes are never the same shape, and the difference can be surprising.

Only a very small portion of the eye is visible, covered as it is by the lids. Eyes tend to sit well back in their sockets, which means that regardless of the direction

Full face view

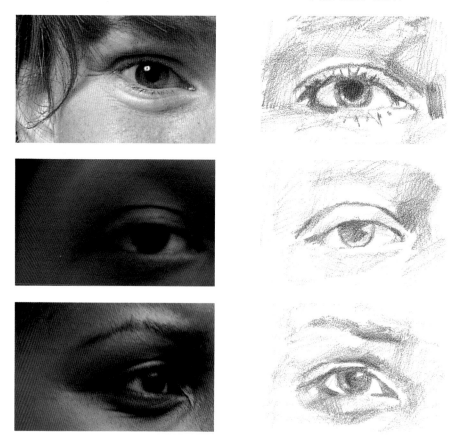

of the light source part, or all, of one or both eyes will be in shadow. The shape and thickness of the brow adds to the density of the cast shadow, as does the skin colour. The shadow and colour on the so-called white of the eye are crucial.

While not always visible, the reflected highlight on the iris gives added life. As the head is turned, the eyes get smaller. They also change in size in relation to each other, the nearer eye looking slightly larger than the further one. From the side it is also possible to see how the eye sits behind the lids. Take care, when painting the head in this position, not to place the eyes too far back in their sockets.

Three-quarter view   Side view

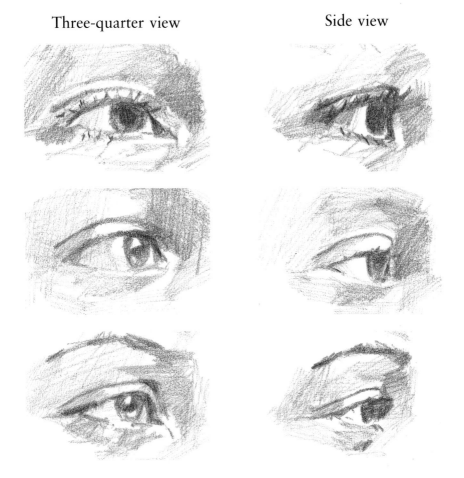

Light Skin   Young

1 For lid and pupil, mix sienna and grey. Add crimson, yellow ochre, and white to mix and use for skin shadows.

1 Umber and grey for dark lids, iris and brow; add red at eye corner; add white and sienna for shadows.

1 Mix grey and crimson for shape of eye; add green to mix for iris. Mix ochre and grey for brow.

2 Mix blue, grey and white for iris. Add white and yellow ochre into skin-shadow mix for mid tones.

2 Mix red, yellow ochre and white for mid tones.

2 Mix orange, crimson and white for mid tones; add grey to this mix for darker part of eye white.

3 Add lemon yellow, crimson and white to mid-tone mix and block in lightest tones, adding more white for highlights. Mix a little iris colour with light skin tone and use for white of eye.

3 Add white and yellow ochre to mid-tone mix and use for lightest skin tones. Add grey into this mix for white of eye. Dot in highlight with pure white.

3 Add white to iris colour for highlight. Mix orange, red and white, with a little iris colour to deaden colour, and use for light skin. Dot in eye highlight with white.

1 *Grey and sienna for brow; add crimson for lid, pupil and creases. Add in white and ochre for darks.*

1 *Mix grey, burnt sienna and a little red for darks of eye, lid and shadow areas.*

1 *Paint brow, pupil and creases with a mix of grey, burnt sienna and crimson.*

2 *Mix blue, white and dark-tone mix for iris. Mix yellow ochre, crimson, blue and white for mid tones.*

2 *Mix umber and grey for eyebrow shadow on lid and beneath eye. Mix red and yellow ochre for mid tones.*

2 *Mix crimson, orange, yellow ochre and white with a touch of green for mid tones.*

3 *Add yellow and white to mid-tone mix and block in lightest tones, working carefully around creases and smile lines. Add iris colour into this mix for white of eye.*

3 *Mix yellow ochre and white with a little red for lightest skin colour. Mix a light grey for white of eye, and dot in highlight with white.*

3 *Lighten mid-tone mix with white, ochre and orange, and use for light tones; add more white for highlights. Add a little green to mix for shadow in eye white.*

Medium Skin

Young

1 *Mix crimson and blue for line of lid. Add raw sienna and black to mix for brow and eye.*

1 *Mix burnt umber and black and use to draw shape of eye and block in darks.*

1 *Mix crimson, raw umber and black and block in darks on lid and brow.*

2 *Mix raw sienna, crimson and blue for mid tones, and add white for opacity. Block in iris with burnt sienna.*

2 *Mix burnt and raw umber, red and white for mid tones.*

2 *Mix crimson, raw sienna, a little yellow and white and block in mid tones.*

3 *Add raw sienna and white to mid-tone mix and block in light skin tones. Add crimson into this at cheekbone and below eye. Mix crimson and blue and touch in at corners of eye.*

3 *Mix red, raw umber and white and block in light tones, adding a little blue into this below eye. Mix red and blue for corners of eye; add white into this for white of eye.*

3 *Mix crimson, raw sienna, yellow and white for the light tones. Use the same mix for corner of eye with white added for highlights.*

1 *Mix crimson and blue for lid and lines. Add black into mix for eye; add raw sienna into mix for brow.*

1 *Mix burnt umber and black for brow and iris. Add red to mix for eye corner, lid and creases.*

1 *Use a mix of black, raw umber and crimson to establish dark lids, brow and shadow beneath eye.*

2 *Mix burnt sienna, raw sienna, crimson and lighten with white, for mid tones.*

2 *Block in mid tones with a mix of red, burnt umber, raw umber and white.*

2 *Block in mid tones with mix of crimson, raw umber, raw sienna and a little white.*

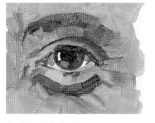

3 *Add raw sienna and crimson into mid-tone mix and block in light tones; modify with white for lightest areas. Use same mix for corner of eye.*

3 *Mix raw umber, burnt umber and white for lightest tones, and add in a little blue below eye. Add more blue plus white for shadow on white of eye. Use light skin colour for reflection in eye.*

3 *Work light skin tones with mix of crimson, raw umber, raw sienna, yellow and white. For shadow in white of eye, add a little black and crimson to light skin mix.*

Dark Skin   Young

1 With a mix of burnt sienna and blue establish basic shape and block in tones above and below eye.

1 Define overall shape with mix of crimson, blue and raw umber. Add more crimson to mix for corner of eye.

1 Blue, burnt sienna on eyelids and brow. Add red to mix for lid and beneath eye.

2 Establish mid tones with mix of burnt sienna and yellow ochre; a little blue will deaden colour.

2 Use mix of raw sienna and crimson to establish mid tone. Add a little blue into mix at side of eye.

2 Blue, burnt sienna and white for shadows. Add red to mix beneath eye and at corner.

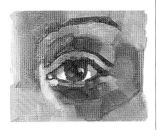

3 Block in lighter tones with mix of burnt sienna and white. Add yellow ochre and white into this for highlights. Mix blue, burnt sienna and white for shadow in white of eye.

3 A mix of white, raw sienna and crimson provides ligher tones above brow and around lower lid. The addition of blue makes grey for white of eye. Dot in highlight with pure white.

3 Lay in lighter tones with mix of raw sienna, blue and red, adding white to give opacity. Add more white to lighten mix for detail on lower lid and highlights.

1 Mix burnt sienna and blue and put in line of lid, skin creases, brow and dark in eye.

1 Mix crimson, blue and raw umber and block in dark shapes. Mix blue and umber for pupil and iris.

1 Block in eye and brow with mix of blue and burnt sienna.

2 Touch in burnt sienna at corner of eye: mix burnt sienna with yellow ochre and block in mid tones.

2 Establish mid tones with crimson and raw sienna knocked back with blue. Apply crimson below and at corner of eye.

2 Add red, raw sienna and blue into previous mix and block in mid tones.

3 Lighten mid-tone mix with white and block in light areas, cutting in carefully around creases in skin. Add ultramarine and white into this mix and put in shadow in white of eye.

3 Working carefully around creases in skin, block in lighter tones with mix of raw sienna, crimson, blue and white. Add a little crimson and blue to white for white of eye.

3 Lighten mid-tone mix with white and burnt sienna for light tones. Touch in red at corner of eye. Use light skin mix with white added for highlights.

MY GRANDMOTHER

Paul Bartlett
25 × 20cm (10 × 8in)

THIS TINY PAINTING has a precious, jewel-like quality about it that reflects the obvious affection the artist feels for the sitter. The portrait is painted on hardboard primed with several coats of traditional gesso, which is more absorbent than the modern, acrylic-based equivalent. Working with small brushes, the artist applies his colours with small strokes and dots, gradually building up the colour and tone, the absorbency of the gesso ground dragging the paint from the brush. The paint is thinned with distilled turpentine, with a little oil medium added for the glazes.

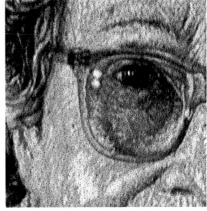

▼ *Cadmium red and cadmium yellow are added to the previous mixture to warm it up for the shadow areas. The artist is greatly concerned with the effects that local and reflected colour have on the tones and colour found in the skin and has glazed the darker areas with these reflected colours.*

▲ *The light falling on the figure picks up and highlights the texture and colour of the old lady's skin. Cool mixes based on titanium white, Naples yellow and yellow ochre are used.*

>19

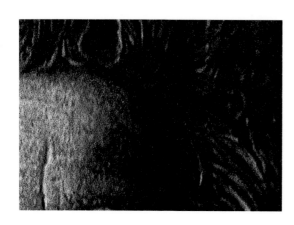

◀ *The blacks are mixed from a selection of browns and blues. Mixing black with darker colours can be effective, whereas mixing black with lighter colours alters their character.*

NOSE

UNLIKE THE MOUTH, the nose takes on a more defined and definite shape as the head is turned to the side. It also seems to get larger or smaller when viewed from different angles. Giving the nose dimension and form when viewed from the front seems to present the most problems, especially when the face is uniformly lit from the front and therefore flat. The following simple tips will help to give character to the nose. When the face is lit from the side and above, the base of the nose

Full face view

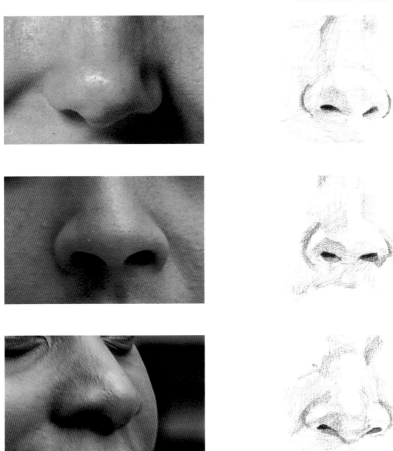

around the nostrils is thrown into deep shadow, with a lighter shadow down one side. The tip of the nose can be made to advance by putting a highlight there. The nose can also be made to project forwards from the face by the shadow it throws onto and across the face. The bridge of the nose can be made to stand out through a contrast with receding, cool, dark shadows within the eye sockets.

Three-quarter view   Side view

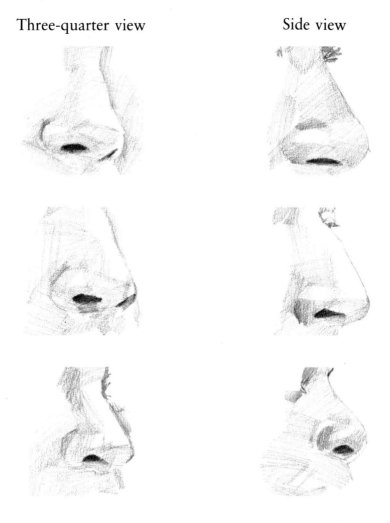

1 Establish darks with red and umber. Darken with blue for nostrils and deep shadow.

1 Mix grey and crimson for dark of nostrils. Add raw sienna and white for shadows.

1 Work darks with sienna and lemon yellow. Add grey to mix for shadow below nose.

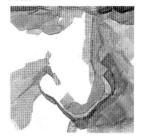

2 For mid tones, lighten dark mix with red, yellow and white.

2 Establish mid tones with mix of crimson, yellow, raw sienna and white.

2 Establish mid tones with varied mixes of red, yellow ochre and white.

3 Add blue to mid-tone mix for shadow beneath nose. Lighten with white, red and yellow for cheeks and side of nose. Leave white ground as highlight on tip of nose.

3 Pale mix of crimson, yellow and white gives lightest tone. Highlight with pure white.

3 Block in lightest tones with mix of cadmium yellow, red and white, adding in a little of the darkest mix to deaden colour. Highlight with pure white.

Middle Aged Noses 23

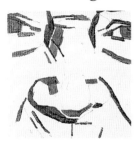

1 *Work darks with umber and blue. Lighten with red for wrinkles and shadow.*

2 *Lighten dark mix with yellow and white to establish mid tones.*

3 *Block in lights with red and yellow mixed with varying amounts of white. Highlights in yellow mixed with white.*

1 *Crimson and sienna for shadows. Add grey to mix for dark of nostrils and shadow.*

2 *Establish lighter tones and shadows with varying mixes of sienna, crimson, yellow and white.*

3 *Mix white and raw sienna for lightest tones. Add a little crimson to this mix and use for pink of nose.*

1 *Establish darks with mix of sienna and grey, lightened with sienna and white for shadows.*

2 *Mix red, yellow ochre and white for mid tones. Add sienna for shadow at side of nose.*

3 *Add white into previous mix for lightest tones. Add a touch of red to the mix and use for pink on end of nose.*

1 *Mix umber and blue for nostrils. Add in yellow, crimson and white for dark tones.*

2 *Mix sienna, yellow and crimson for mid tones. Add in blue beneath nose and eyes.*

3 *Establish light tones with mix of yellow and white.*

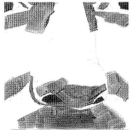

1 *Umber and blue for nostrils. Add red and sienna for darks; add blue beneath nose.*

2 *For mid tones, add more red plus yellow to dark mix.*

3 *Mix raw sienna and yellow for light tones; lighten with white for highlights.*

1 *Mix grey and sienna for nostrils. Mix sienna, crimson and ochre for darks.*

2 *Mix sienna and ochre for mid tones; add ochre and crimson to this for cheeks.*

3 *Mix yellow ochre, white and crimson for the lightest tones, adding in more white for highlights.*

1 *Mix umber, crimson and blue for nostrils. Mix sienna, crimson and umber for darkest tones.*

2 *Crimson and sienna mix gives mid tones. Draw in wrinkles and shadow beneath nose.*

3 *Block in light tones using mix of sienna and yellow. Add white into this mix and use for highlights.*

1 *Red and sienna for darks. Add umber and blue to mix for shadow below nose.*

2 *Establish mid tones with varying mixes of sienna, red and blue.*

3 *Block in lightest tones with mix of raw sienna and yellow, lightened with white for highlights.*

1 *Establish form and dark tones with mixes of grey, sienna and crimson.*

2 *Varying mixes of burnt sienna, yellow ochre and crimson give mid tones.*

3 *Lighten mid-tone mix with white and yellow ochre for lightest tones.*

Dark Skin   Young

1 Mix red and grey for
nostrils. To this, add orange,
ochre and red for darks.

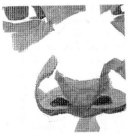

2 Add Naples yellow and a
little red into mix; deaden
with a little grey.

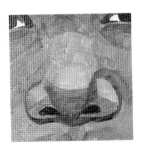

3 Add Naples yellow,
orange and a little red to
previous mix for lightest
tones. Add white and Naples
yellow into this and use for
highlights.

1 Mix umber, crimson and
blue for nostrils. Mix
crimson, orange and sienna
for shadows.

2 Mix sienna and crimson
with a little blue and white
for mid tones.

3 Mix orange, raw sienna
and white for lightest tones.
Add a little blue to mix for
highlight. Darken nostrils
with mix of raw umber and
blue.

1 Mix burnt sienna and
blue for nostrils. Mix in
more sienna for dark tones.

2 Establish mid tones by
adding burnt sienna and
yellow into dark mix.

3 Mix yellow with a little
mid-tone mix for light tones.

1 *Block in nostrils and darkest tones with mix of red and grey.*

1 *Mix umber, crimson and blue for darks. Add a little orange for shape of nose.*

1 *Mix blue and burnt sienna for darks.*

2 *Red, orange and yellow ochre deadened with grey give mid tones.*

2 *Sienna, orange, crimson and white with a little blue give mid tones.*

2 *Modify dark mix with more burnt sienna and yellow ochre for mid tones.*

3 *Mix orange, Naples yellow and yellow ochre for lighter tones, and lighten with white for highlight.*

3 *Add white to mid-tone mix for light tone. For highlights use white, a little light-tone mix and blue.*

3 *Add yellow into a little of the dark mix for lightest tones. Add blue into mix and use for highlights.*

THE ITALIAN CONNECTION

Olwyn Tarrant
75 × 62.5cm (30 × 25in)

THE PRIMED CANVAS is stained with a thin, light mix of burnt sienna. Once this is dry, the subject is drawn in with a darker mix of burnt sienna, using a thin bristle brush. Using large bristle brushes, the artist then blocks in the planes of tone and colour that give the image form and structure. The palette of colours relates to the background and the overall desired ambience.

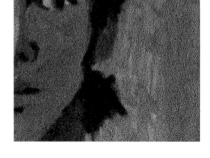

▲ *The warm, light skin tones are mixed from cadmium red, Indian yellow, yellow ochre and titanium white.*

▲ *The light tones are modified with ultramarine blue, alizarin crimson, blue black and raw sienna.*

◀ *The hair is worked with loose strokes of burnt sienna, blue/black, and a grey mixed by adding white to a blue/brown mix.*

MOUTH

ALONG WITH THE eyes, the mouth gives expression to the face. The complex muscle group that serves to animate the mouth is connected to and has a direct influence on the chin, cheeks and nose, and so the rest of the face. Even a slight alteration in the shape of the mouth can change the look or apparent temperament of the sitter. The lips are not flat, but curl away and stand proud of the face. This can be seen more easily from the side. The upper lip usually appears darker than the lower lip because its main surface is angled slightly downwards.

Full face view

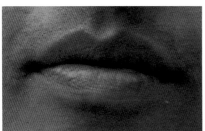

The lower lip is lighter in tone because it catches more light. When the lips are held together, the shadow where they join forms the line of the mouth. This line disappears once the mouth is opened slightly. Viewed from the side, the lips are often very small – sometimes almost non-existent, and it can be difficult to get the size and shape right from this angle. This is often more easily accomplished if the mouth is slightly open. It is important to note that there is no line around the lips, just a change in colour and tone.

Three-quarter view   Side view

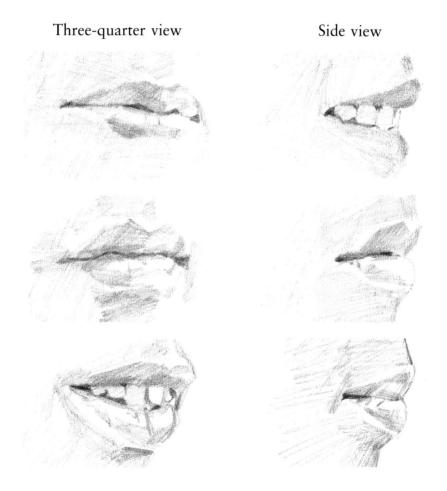

1 Define lip line with mix of grey and red. Mix red and blue for shadows.

1 Mix crimson, blue and raw umber for lips. Add raw sienna and white into mix for teeth.

1 Define mouth shape and lips with mix of red, raw sienna and grey.

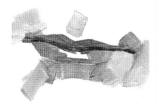

2 Mix red, yellow ochre and white for lip colour. Add white and yellow ochre to this mix and block in skin.

2 Mix crimson, raw sienna and white for mid tone on lips. Add raw umber and blue into mix for shadows.

2 Establish lips and gums with mix of red, raw sienna and white. Add blue to mix for darker skin passage.

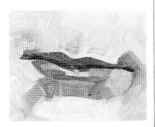

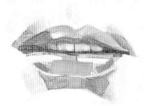

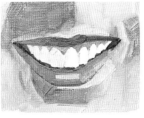

3 Add white into basic lip colour and put in highlights. Mix yellow ochre, red and white for palest skin colour.

3 Establish lip highlights with mix of raw sienna, crimson and white. Add a little more raw sienna into mix and block in skin.

3 Block in teeth with raw sienna, grey and white. Mix lightest skin tone from red, raw sienna and white.

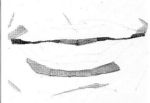

1 *Define lip line with red and blue mix. Add yellow ochre and white and block in dark skin tones.*

1 *Define shape with mix of crimson, blue and raw umber. Add white and raw sienna into mix for shadow.*

1 *Mix blue, grey, red, raw sienna and white in varying proportions and define darks in and around mouth.*

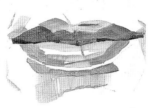
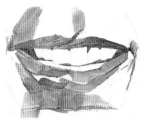

2 *Mix red, yellow ochre and white for lips. Add ochre, grey and white and block in skin mid tones.*

2 *Crimson, raw sienna and white give a range of lip pinks. Add blue into mix for shadows.*

2 *Lighten lip colour with red, raw sienna and white. Introduce blue to this mix and block in skin mid tones.*

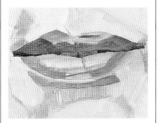
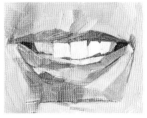

3 *Mix red, yellow ochre and white in varying proportions for light skin passages and highlights along edge of lower lip.*

3 *Block in lightest tones with pale mix of white and raw sienna, with a little lip pink added. Use same mix for highlight on lower lip.*

3 *Work darker teeth with grey, raw sienna and white. Mix raw sienna and white for skin, cooled with blue, which also helps give a transparent look to the skin.*

1 *Use grey and red to define opening. A mix of red, raw umber and raw sienna gives darker lip tone.*

1 *Paint the line of mouth in mix of grey and burnt umber. Mix red, raw sienna and white for dark of lips.*

1 *Paint line of mouth with mix of crimson and grey. Add crimson, orange and white and use for lips.*

2 *Block in lip colour with mix of red, sienna and white. Add yellow and umber and use for shadows.*

2 *Mix grey, burnt umber, white and some of dark lip mix and use for shadows and stubble around mouth.*

2 *Add orange, raw sienna and white into lip colour for skin mid tone.*

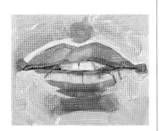

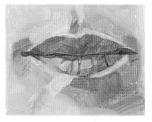

3 *Add raw sienna, yellow and white into lip colour for light tone. Add more white and yellow and use for pale line over lip. Add grey into mix and use for teeth.*

3 *Lighten previous mix with yellow, raw sienna and white and use to block in skin.*

3 *Mix crimson and orange for light red on upper lip; add white into this and use for lower lip pinks. Lighten mid skin-tone mix with raw sienna and white and use for lightest tones.*

1 *Define lip line with mix of red and grey. Mix red and raw umber and block in lips.*

1 *Define shape with grey, burnt umber and raw sienna. Add white into mix and use for shadows at side.*

1 *Block in creases in skin, line of mouth and shadows with mix of crimson and grey.*

2 *Mix red, raw sienna and white for lighter lip colour. Add grey into this mix and use for shadows on skin.*

2 *Introduce more raw sienna, red and white for skin tones. Add more red and white for light on lip.*

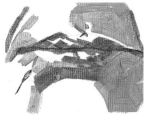

2 *Add crimson and orange into previous mix and use for lips. Add white and raw sienna for skin mid tone.*

3 *Add white to lip colour and use for lower lip highlights. Block in rest of skin with a mix of lip colour, sienna, yellow and white.*

3 *Mix raw sienna, yellow, red and white and block in lightest skin tones. Add in grey to knock back colour on chin and upper lip.*

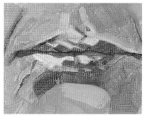

3 *Introduce highlights to lips with mid tone mixed with crimson and white. Lighten mid-tone mix with raw sienna, orange and white and use for lightest skin passages.*

1 Mix grey and burnt sienna for dark of mouth. Mix blue and crimson for lip colour.

1 Suggest lips and line of mouth with mix of red, blue and raw sienna.

1 Mix blue and burnt sienna for mouth line; add burnt sienna and yellow ochre for dark of lips.

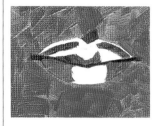

2 Redden lips with crimson, burnt sienna and white. Add raw sienna and blue to this and use for skin mid tone.

2 Strengthen lips with mix of red and burnt sienna. Mix burnt sienna and blue for areas of shadow.

2 Add blue and white into mix and use for overall skin tone. Tonal range is limited.

3 Mix raw sienna, burnt sienna and white and add a little blue for lighter tones. Highlight lips with crimson and white. Block in teeth using white mixed with light skin colour.

3 Mix yellow and burnt sienna for edge of mouth. Add white and a little blue into this mix and use for rest of skin. Mix red, blue and white for lip highlights.

3 Add yellow ochre and white into previous mix and use for lip colour and area above top lip.

1 *Establish darks in mouth and on lips with mix of grey, crimson and burnt sienna.*

1 *Mix blue, red and raw sienna for dark of lips and mouth line.*

1 *Mix blue and burnt sienna for mouth line; add crimson for dark of lips.*

2 *Define lips using mix of crimson, raw sienna, blue and white. Mix burnt sienna and white for skin mid tone.*

2 *Lighten the mix with yellow and white for upper lip. Mix blue and burnt sienna for darks to use around mouth.*

2 *Mix crimson, blue and yellow ochre for mouth line; add more crimson into mix for dark in lips.*

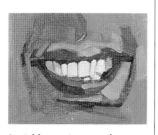

3 *Add raw sienna and white to skin mid-tone mix for lighter skin. Mix crimson and white for highlight on lips; add blue into this and use for grey base for teeth.*

3 *Add white into upper-lip colour and use for highlights; add yellow into this mix and use for lights around mouth. Mix burnt sienna, yellow and white for skin colour.*

3 *Lighten previous mix with crimson, yellow ochre and white for lightest skin passages. Add blue to mix and use beneath mouth. Add more white and yellow ochre for lights around mouth.*

38

FLOELLA BENJAMIN

June Mendoza
154 × 76cm (65 × 30in)

THE SHAPE AND FORMAT of the canvas were chosen to match the elegant stance of the slim model. Painted with loose, yet considered brushwork, the painting is predominantly cool with a few warmer tones in the shadows of the face, dress and jacket.

▶ *Yellow ochre, alizarin crimson and white with a little ultramarine blue added give the reddish-browns on the lit side of the face. The mid tones are warmed by the addition of cadmium red and yellow.*

▲ *Only the reflections in the eyes are put in with pure white. The so-called whites of the eyes are mixed from skin tones, white and grey.*

◀ *A dark blue-grey mix is brushed in under the chin and down the neck, indicating the effect of the reflected light from the pink dress.*

EARS ARE OFTEN hidden by hair, or are in deep shadow or concealed by the angle of view. The ears grow out of the side of the head – they are not stuck on – the front of the ear should flow into the side of the face without a break. The ears are fixed. They cannot change position or shape by muscle action, unlike the eyes, nose and mouth. However, they do change dramatically as the angle of view is altered. Depending on the position they are seen from, ears can look completely wrong so

Full face view

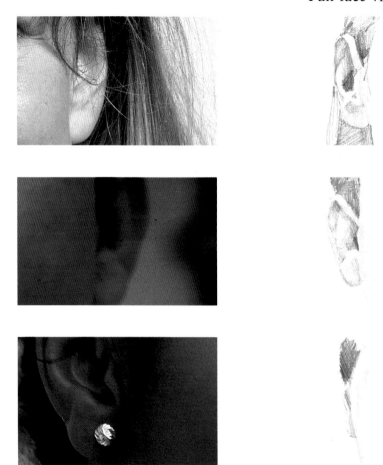

it is important to observe them objectively. Large ears that lie flat and close to the head will lose their ear-like shape when seen from the front, whereas smaller ears that lie at more of an angle to the head will be seen to retain their shape when viewed from the front. Ears are usually a deeper colour than the rest of the face due to blood circulation and the effect of shadows within the folds of the ear.

Three-quarter view   Side view

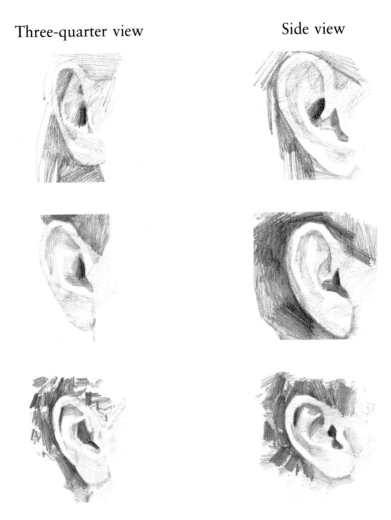

Light Skin

Young

1 Mix raw umber, red and blue for darks.

1 Mix grey and burnt sienna for darks. Add crimson for folds of ear.

1 Mix blue and sienna for darks. Lighten mix with crimson and ochre to describe shape.

2 Mix yellow ochre, red and white for mid tones.

2 Mix burnt sienna and white with a little crimson for mid tones.

2 Add white to dark mix for mid tones.

3 Add white and a little blue into mid-tone mix and block in lightest tones.

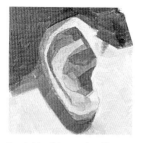

3 Add white and yellow to mid-tone mix for lighter tones. Continue to add white for highlights.

3 Modify mid-tone mix with lemon yellow and additional white for light skin tones and highlights.

1 *Block in darks with varying mixes of raw umber, red and blue.*

2 *Mix yellow ochre, red and white plus a little blue for the mid tones.*

3 *Modify mid-tone mix with white and use for lightest tones.*

1 *Mix grey, burnt sienna and crimson and use for darkest tones.*

2 *Add crimson and yellow into dark mix for mid tones.*

3 *Mix white and yellow with a hint of mid-tone mix for highlights.*

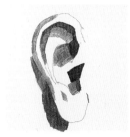

1 *Mix blue and burnt sienna for darks. Lighten with ochre and crimson to describe shape.*

2 *Modify dark mix with crimson, lemon yellow and white for mid tones.*

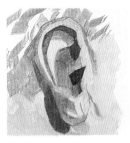

3 *Lighten mid-tone mix with white and a little yellow ochre, and a touch of blue for light skin tones.*

1 *Mix burnt umber and blue for darks and suggestion of general shape.*

1 *Mix blue and umber for darks. Add red to mix for shadow behind ear.*

1 *Mix raw umber, red and blue for darks.*

2 *Mix red and yellow with white and a little blue for mid tones.*

2 *Add yellow ochre and red to dark mix for mid tones.*

2 *Mix red, ochre, white and a little dark mix for mid tone.*

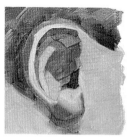

3 *Add a little yellow and white into mid-tone mix and use for lightest skin tones.*

3 *Mix yellow ochre and red for lightest tones and add a little mid-tone mix to knock back colour.*

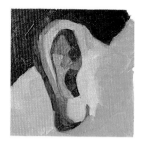

3 *Mix yellow ochre and red with a little white for lightest tone. Add in extra white for highlights.*

1 *Mix blue, burnt umber and a little red for darkest tones.*

2 *Mix red and yellow with hint of dark mix to deaden colour for mid tones.*

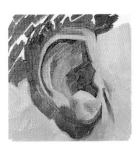

3 *Lighten mid-tone mix with white and use for lightest skin tones.*

1 *Mix red and umber for shadows within and behind ear. Add in blue for darks.*

2 *Lighten mix with ochre and red, adding white to mix for opacity, for mid tones.*

3 *Mix yellow ochre and white and add in a little dark mix, and use for lightest tones.*

1 *Mix umber and blue for darks. Add red to mix for inside ear.*

2 *Mix red and yellow ochre for mid tone.*

3 *Add white and yellow ochre into mid-tone mix and use for lightest tones and highlights.*

1 *For darkest tones of inner ear mix grey and burnt sienna.*

1 *Mix blue, burnt sienna and crimson for the darkest tone.*

1 *Mix burnt umber, blue and crimson for darkest tones.*

2 *Mix burnt sienna, raw sienna and white with a little red for mid tones.*

2 *Add crimson and raw sienna into dark mix for mid tones.*

2 *Mix yellow ochre, crimson and blue for mid tones.*

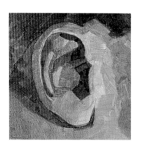

3 *Add raw sienna and white into mid-tone mix and use for lighter tones. Modify with grey and burnt sienna for duller colour. Lighten mix with white and use for lightest tones.*

3 *Add white and raw sienna to mid tone and use for light tones. Add a little blue and white to mix for highlights.*

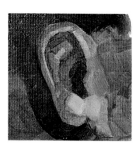

3 *Add orange and white to mid tone and use for light passages. Mix this colour with white and blue and use for highlight colour.*

1 *Mix grey and burnt sienna for darks.*

1 *Mix burnt sienna, crimson and blue and block in darks.*

1 *Mix burnt umber, crimson and blue for dark tones.*

2 *Add burnt sienna, raw sienna and red into dark mix for mid tones.*

2 *Lighten dark mix with raw sienna and white; add crimson and burnt sienna.*

2 *Add yellow ochre, crimson and blue to mix and block in mid tones.*

3 *Add raw sienna and white into mid-tone mix and use for lightest tones. Bright colour can be subdued by adding a little grey.*

3 *Add raw sienna and white to mid-tone mix and use for lightest tones and highlights.*

3 *Add orange and crimson into mid-tone mix and use for lighter tones. Add in yellow ochre and white with a little blue and use for highlights.*

LYDIA

Ian Sidaway
135 × 112.5cm (54 × 45in)

STRONG MORNING LIGHT pouring through a window to one side casts one side of the figure into warm shadow that is full of tone and colour. Colour has been bleached out on the side towards the light, so that side is painted in a less complex way with flatter colour. The contour on the lit side of the face is hinted at by the cast shadow from one of the glazing bars on the unseen windows. Painted over a detailed drawing on a white ground, the portrait shows how strong directional light can give drama and added interest to a straightforward pose. The dark, uniform background serves to intensify the colour on the figure and focuses the eye on the subject.

▶ *The skin colour on the side towards the light is painted using a cool mix of lemon yellow, alizarin crimson, a little cobalt blue and plenty of titanium white.*

◀ *The highlights on the hair are created by painting carefully around them, leaving the white ground to show through.*

▲ *On the leg beneath the skirt, the quality of the colour comes not only from shadow, but also from light passing through the coloured materials. The tones are warmed with cadmium red and cadmium yellow.*

PULLING IT TOGETHER

FORM AND SHAPE are given to the head and face by the underlying shape of the skull, which is covered by a very thin layer of muscle. You can feel the contours of the skull and jaw quite clearly beneath the skin, which is not the case with other bones in the body. Skull shape varies from individual to individual, and there are distinct differences between ethnic groups. As the skull shape dictates the way our features are arranged, the variations in shape between one person and another explain why no two people look exactly alike. As a general rule, facial features in the young tend to be rounder and fuller. With age, the features become angular. The bones of the skull show more clearly beneath the surface as weight is lost and the skin begins to loose its firmness and tone.

With pale skin the shadows are cool, while in areas that are brightly lit the colour is warmer. The reverse is true of dark skin.

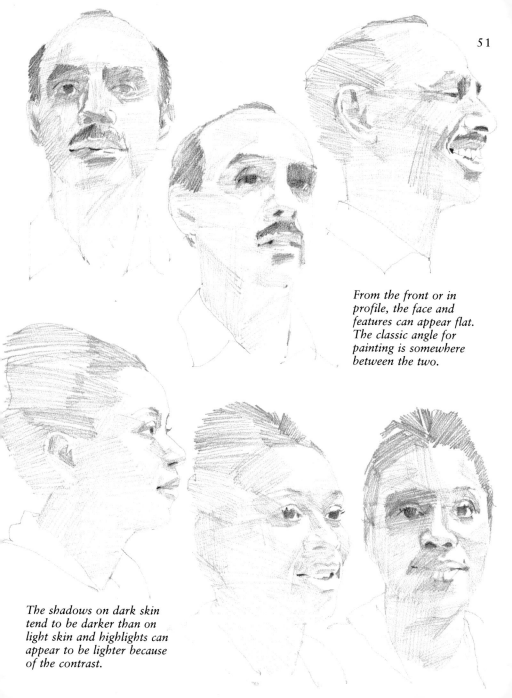

From the front or in profile, the face and features can appear flat. The classic angle for painting is somewhere between the two.

The shadows on dark skin tend to be darker than on light skin and highlights can appear to be lighter because of the contrast.

Light Skin Young

1 *Grey and raw umber for very dark tones; lighten for hair. Warmer mix for forehead and neck.*

4 *Mix crimson, yellow and white and block in mid tones on forehead, nose, cheeks and chin.*

5 *Crimson, yellow and white for lightest skin tones with white added for highlights.*

2 *Crimson, blue, raw sienna and white mixes for shadows. Crimson, raw sienna and white for lips.*

3 *Mix mid tone shadows with crimson, raw sienna, raw umber and white.*

6 *Sienna, yellow and white for light tones and highlights on hair. Alizarin and blue for shadow on sweater; add white for rest of sweater.*

1 *Blue, raw umber and white for dark tones in hair. Add crimson for the darkest shadows.*

4 *Mix raw sienna, yellow and white plus previous mix and block in rest of mid tones.*

5 *Add white to mid-tone mix for lights; extra white and grey for teeth.*

2 *Add burnt sienna and white to previous mix for wrinkles; add blue and crimson for darker tones.*

3 *Raw sienna, crimson, white and yellow for mid tones; more yellow for lips.*

6 *Block in lights in hair with mix of white, grey and yellow ochre. Mix burnt sienna, raw sienna and white mix, for dress.*

Medium Skin Young

1 *Use grey and burnt sienna for hair and lids; add more sienna for eye, nostrils and mouth. Lighten with ochre.*

4 *Add white, ochre, lemon yellow into mix for mid tones, white and blue for lighter passage.*

5 *Add white to mid-tone mix for lightest areas. Mix white, ochre and grey for eye 'whites'.*

2 *Add more ochre for neck and face, add in red and blue for dark in lips.*

3 *Add ochre and white into mix for darker mid tones; add red for lips and face.*

6 *Mix grey, a little blue and white and use for highlight on hair.*

1 Mix grey, white and lemon yellow for grey hair; mix grey, red and sienna for darks.

4 Dark mix, ochre, red, white for mid tones. Lip mix, blue and white for grey tones.

5 Add white and lemon into previous mix for light tones, cutting around wrinkles and darker tones.

2 Add red and blue into mix for dark tones in wrinkles and on side of face.

3 Add red and ochre to mix for shadows. Mix red, blue, white, dark mix for lips.

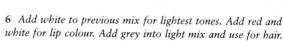

6 Add white to previous mix for lightest tones. Add red and white for lip colour. Add grey into light mix and use for hair.

Dark Skin

Young

1 *Blue and burnt sienna for darkest areas; add burnt sienna and white to mix for shadows.*

4 *Add raw sienna, yellow and white to previous mix for rest of mid tones.*

5 *Add white and yellow into mix for light tone; more yellow and white for highlight.*

2 *Raw sienna, crimson and dark mix for dark tones. Add crimson for mouth, nose and eyes.*

3 *Add burnt sienna, yellow and white for mid tones. Add crimson, white for lips.*

6 *Mix white with a little light skin colour for teeth and white of eye. Add grey to this mix and use for lightest hair.*

1 *Blue and burnt sienna for eyes, nose and mouth. Add more blue for neck and stubble.*

4 *For grey hair add white and grey into mid-tone mix.*

5 *Add raw sienna, yellow and white into mid-tone mix for light tones.*

2 *Mix burnt and raw sienna and white for rest of darker tones. Add crimson for lips.*

3 *Mix burnt and raw sienna, crimson and white for mid tones across face.*

6 *Add white to light skin mix and use for highlights. Use light skin tone in eyes and add white for highnote on lips.*

1 Establish darks using flowing strokes mixed from raw umber, yellow ochre and grey.

1 Block in mid-tone mass with mix of burnt umber and burnt sienna.

1 Block in darks with mix of red, burnt umber and orange.

2 Add a little yellow and white to previous mix for mid tones.

2 Add grey to mid-tone mix and work into mid tones to establish darks.

2 Mix orange, white and red for mid tones.

3 Add more white to mid-tone mix for lightest strands of hair, blending with fluid strokes into mid tones.

3 Mix white and Naples yellow and draw in lightest strands of hair.

3 Add white and yellow to mid-tone mix for highlights.

1 *Establish darks with quick strokes of raw umber, yellow ochre and grey.*

1 *Block in darks with varying mixes of grey, raw umber and raw sienna.*

1 *Block in darks with mix of red, burnt umber and orange.*

2 *Mix yellow ochre, raw umber and white for mid tones.*

2 *Lighten dark mix with yellow ochre, white and Naples yellow and block in mid tones following wave of hair.*

2 *Add orange and yellow to dark mix for mid tones. Keep brushstrokes fairly dry so that light of support shows through.*

3 *Redefine a few darks with mix of raw umber and grey. Flick in highlights using white mixed with touches of cadmium and yellow ochre.*

3 *Suggest lightest strands of hair by scratching out individual strands in wet paint with scalpel blade.*

3 *Lighten mid-tone mix with white and yellow and put in highlights. Use end of brush to scratch out individual strands of hair.*

Medium Skin

Young

1 *Mix a dark brown from blue and burnt sienna for darks.*

1 *Mix grey and burnt sienna and block in darks with short, angled strokes.*

1 *Block in darks with mix of burnt umber and blue.*

2 *Add burnt sienna and yellow ochre to dark mix for mid tones.*

2 *Add yellow ochre into dark mix and cut in mid tones.*

2 *Add white and yellow ochre to dark mix for mid tones.*

3 *Brush on yellow ochre without blending for lightest tone.*

3 *Add white to mid-tone mix and chop in highlights with direct strokes. Do not blend.*

3 *Add white and blue into mid-tone mix for lights. Draw in a few individual hairs.*

1 Mix blue and burnt sienna for darkest hair and shadows.

1 Establish darks with mix of burnt sienna and grey.

1 Mix white, burnt umber and blue for darker patches of grey hair.

2 Mix yellow ochre, burnt sienna and a little blue for mid tones.

2 Add yellow ochre into dark mix for mid tones.

2 Add white and yellow ochre to dark mix and block in mid tones.

3 Thin mid-tone mix for lightest tones. Add a few 'grey' hairs by scratching them out with a scalpel.

3 Add white into mid-tone mix and paint in lighter tones. Use handle of brush to scratch in a few greying hairs.

3 Add white and a little blue into mid-tone mix and put in lightest tone.

1 Mix burnt sienna and blue and block in dark areas, following curl of hair with brushstrokes.

1 Mix blue and burnt sienna and paint in with fluid strokes.

1 Establish mid tones with mix of burnt umber and blue.

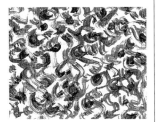

2 Add raw sienna and white into dark mix and brush in mid tones with twisting strokes.

2 Add orange and white into dark mix. Thin mixture and brush it over dark strokes for mid-tone areas.

2 Add ivory black into mid-tone and block in darks.

3 Mix titanium white into mid-tone mix, add a little blue, and block in highlights.

3 Add blue and plenty of white into mid-tone mix and put in highlights.

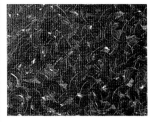

3 Scratch in individual hairs with a scalpel blade.

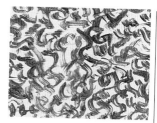

1 *Mix blue and burnt sienna for mid-tone curls.*

1 *Establish darks with mix of blue and burnt sienna, painting in whispy, flowing strokes.*

1 *Apply a thin, dry mix of blue and burnt umber for mid tones.*

2 *Darken mid-tone mix with blue and put in dark centres to curls.*

2 *Add orange into dark mix for mid tones, and loosely brush this over darks, allowing white ground to show through as grey hair.*

2 *Add black into mid-tone mix and block in darks with thin, curly strokes, allowing white support to show through.*

3 *Add blue and white into mix and put in lightest tone. Leave the white ground to show as lightest grey hairs.*

3 *Add white into mid-tone mix and put in highlights.*

3 *Work over hair, scratching in lights and individual grey hairs.*

Colour Chart

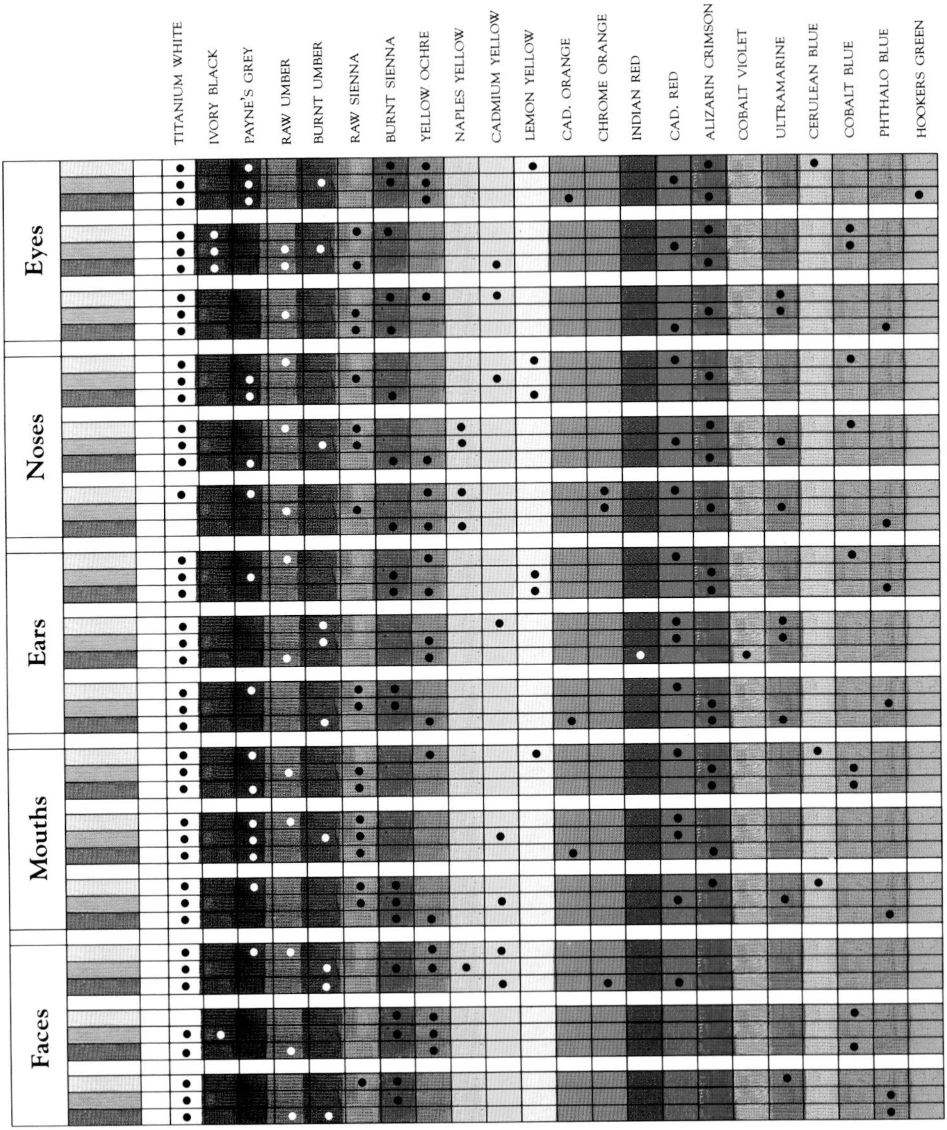
TITANIUM WHITE
IVORY BLACK
PAYNE'S GREY
RAW UMBER
BURNT UMBER
RAW SIENNA
BURNT SIENNA
YELLOW OCHRE
NAPLES YELLOW
CADMIUM YELLOW
LEMON YELLOW
CAD. ORANGE
CHROME ORANGE
INDIAN RED
CAD. RED
ALIZARIN CRIMSON
COBALT VIOLET
ULTRAMARINE
CERULEAN BLUE
COBALT BLUE
PHTHALO BLUE
HOOKERS GREEN
Eyes
Noses
Ears
Mouths
Faces

This
Treasure Cove Story
belongs to

I AM ARIEL

A CENTUM BOOK 978-1-912841-36-3
Published in Great Britain by Centum Books Ltd.
This edition published 2019.

1 3 5 7 9 10 8 6 4 2

Centum Books Ltd, 20 Devon Square, Newton Abbot, Devon, TQ12 2HR, UK.
9/10 Fenian St, Dublin 2, D02 RX24, Ireland.

www.centumbooksltd.co.uk | books@centumbooksltd.co.uk
CENTUM BOOKS Limited Reg. No. 07641486.

A CIP catalogue record for this book is available
from the British Library.

Printed in China.

DISNEY
PRINCESS

THE LITTLE MERMAID

I Am Ariel

By Andrea Posner-Sanchez
Illustrated by Alan Batson

I am
Ariel.

I live under the sea in the kingdom of

Atlantica.

My father is King Triton.
He rules all the **merpeople**.

I have six sisters. Their names are *Alana, Aquata, Andrina, Attina, Arista* and *Adella*.

I'm the youngest.

Being a mermaid is fun! I get to sing with the **royal orchestra,**

conducted by *Sebastian* the crab...

... and go exploring with my best friend, *Flounder.*

Do you want to know
a secret?

As much fun as it is to
be a **mermaid**, I'd really
rather be
human!

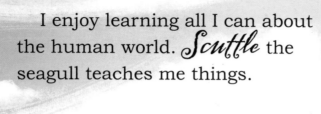

I enjoy learning all I can about the human world. *Scuttle* the seagull teaches me things.

Sometimes, even though I am not supposed to, I swim to the surface to watch humans.

I think humans are wonderful. Especially the one called *Prince Eric*!

I like to **collect objects** I find
in **shipwrecks**. All my treasures used
to belong to humans.

I don't get scared easily – not around sharks,

eels...

or even Ursula, the sea witch

When I want something badly enough,
I don't give up.

I made a deal with Ursula.
In exchange for my voice, she
made me human for a few days.

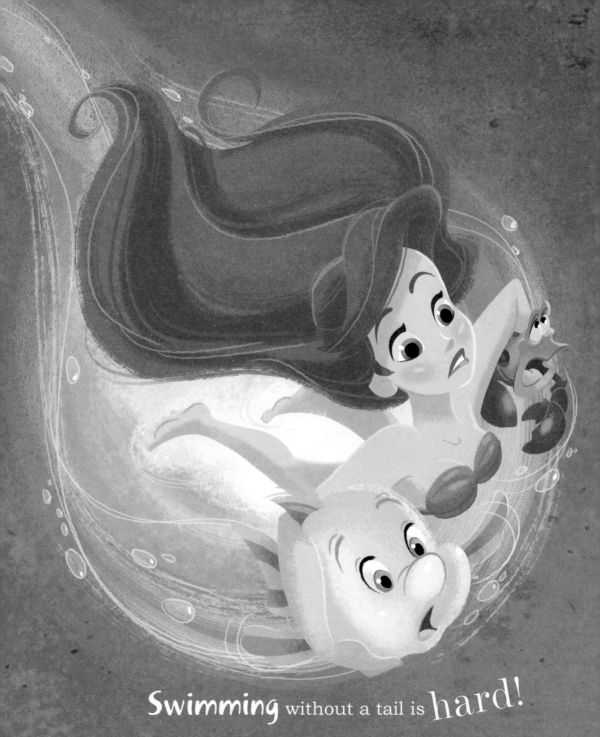

Swimming without a tail is hard!

I **love** my new legs!

I'm glad Scuttle
showed me the proper
way to use a
dinglehopper!

I learned that you don't need to speak
to fall in love...

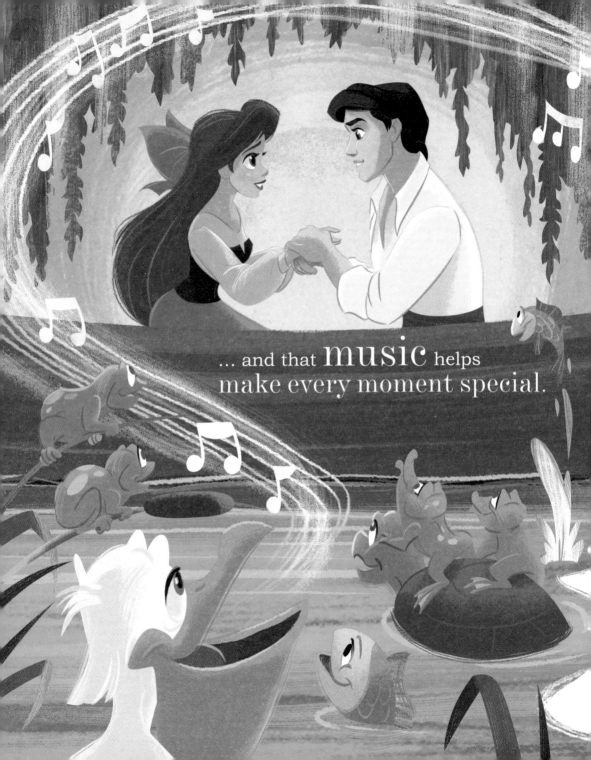

... and that **music** helps make every moment special.

I am so thankful my father used his magical trident to make me human... this time forever.

I get to be with Eric and still stay close to my merfamily. Now I have the **best of both worlds**!

Treasure Cove Stories

Please contact Centum Books
to receive the full list of titles in
the *Treasure Cove Stories* series.
books@centumbooksltd.co.uk

Classic favourites

1 Three Little Pigs
2 Snow White and
the Seven Dwarfs
3 The Fox and the Hound
- Hide-and-Seek
4 Dumbo
5 Cinderella
6 Cinderella's Friends
7 Alice in Wonderland
8 Mad Hatter's Tea Party
from Alice in Wonderland
9 Mickey Mouse and
his Spaceship
10 Peter Pan
11 Pinocchio
12 Mickey and the Beanstalk
13 Sleeping Beauty
and the Good Fairies
14 The Lucky Puppy
15 Chicken Little
16 The Incredibles
17 Coco
18 Winnie the Pooh and Tigger
19 The Sword in the Stone
20 Mary Poppins
21 The Jungle Book
22 The Aristocats
23 Lady and the Tramp
24 Bambi
25 Bambi - Friends of the Forest

Recently published

50 Frozen
51 Cinderella is my Babysitter
52 Beauty and the Beast
- I am the Beast
53 Blaze and the Monster Machines
- Mighty Monster Machines
54 Blaze and the Monster Machines
- Dino Parade!
55 Teenage Mutant Ninja Turtles
- Follow the Ninja!

56 I am a Princess
57 The Big Book of Paw Patrol
58 Paw Patrol
- Adventures with Grandpa!
59 Paw Patrol - Pirate Pups!
60 Trolls
61 Trolls Holiday
62 The Secret Life of Pets
63 Zootropolis
64 Ariel is my Babysitter
65 Tiana is my Babysitter
66 Belle is my Babysitter
67 Paw Patrol
- Itty-Bitty Kitty Rescue
68 Moana
69 Nella the Princess Knight
- My Heart is Bright!
70 Guardians of the Galaxy
71 Captain America
- High-Stakes Heist!
72 Ant-Man
73 The Mighty Avengers
74 The Mighty Avengers
- Lights Out!
75 The Incredible Hulk
76 Shimmer & Shine
- Wish Upon a Sleepover
77 Shimmer & Shine - Backyard Ballet
78 Paw Patrol - All-Star Pups!
79 Teenage Mutant Ninja Turtles
- Really Spaced Out!
80 I am Ariel
81 Madagascar
82 Jasmine is my Babysitter
83 How to Train your Dragon
84 Shrek
85 Puss in Boots
86 Kung Fu Panda
87 Beauty and the Beast - I am Belle
88 The Lion Guard
- The Imaginary Okapi
89 Thor - Thunder Strike!
90 Guardians of the Galaxy
- Rocket to the Rescue!
91 Nella the Princess Knight
- Nella and the Dragon
92 Shimmer & Shine
- Treasure Twins!

93 Olaf's Frozen Adventure
94 Black Panther
95 Trolls
- Branch's Bunker Birthday
96 Trolls - Poppy's Party
97 The Ugly Duckling
98 Cars - Look Out for Mater!
99 101 Dalmatians
100 The Sorcerer's Apprentice
101 Tangled
102 Avengers
- The Threat of Thanos
103 Puppy Dog Pals
- Don't Rain on my Pug-Rade
104 Jurassic Park
105 The Mighty Thor
106 Doctor Strange

Latest publications

107 Captain Marvel
108 The Invincible Iron Man
109 Black Panther
- Warriors of Wakanda
110 The Big Freeze
111 Ratatouille
112 Aladdin
113 Aladdin - I am the Genie
114 Seven Dwarfs Find a House
115 Toy Story
116 Toy Story 4
117 Paw Patrol - Jurassic Bark!
118 Paw Patrol
- Mighty Pup Power!
119 Shimmer & Shine
- Pet Talent Show!
120 SpongeBob SquarePants
- Krabby Patty Caper
121 The Lion King - I am Simba
122 Winnie the Pooh
- The Honey Tree
123 Frozen II
124 Baby Shark and the
Colours of the Ocean
125 Baby Shark and
the Police Sharks!
126 Trolls World Tour

Book list may be subject to change.